Flower photography.
- Tips, tricks and simple editing methods.

by JAYARAM A S

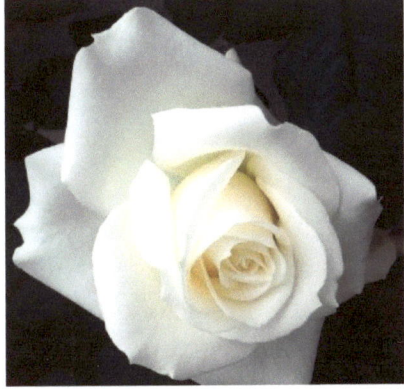

Among many types of photography, flower photography is a very important one. Whatever maybe special field of photography of any photographer, he will have a large amount of flower photograph collections with him. In that context I have explained in detail, the method of taking flower pictures. For any type of photography, fundamentals are required. Hence I have explained basic camera settings and fundamentals of photography.

I have classified the flowers into three important categories as:

- Small flowers
- Medium size flowers and
- Large flowers.

In small flowers almost any camera will do and camera settings are of less importance even though it is required. Normally these flowers are in groups and photographs are also in large collection of flowers arranged in different ways.

It is medium size flowers that are extremely important, as rose, dahlia and others are in this category. In this category I have explained in detail with camera settings, how a photograph of the flower is clicked. Important parameters like background light, composition, direction of light, camera angle, exposure and composition.

Large flower, each camera setting is critical. Also in this category light variations, depth of field and tricks like sprinkling some water on flower, so that the flower can have reflections of water droplets on petals. I have also included the method of extreme close up of hibiscus.

These are the days of digital world and most of the corrections are done by editing photos. Therefore I have explained in detail, simple editing used Microsoft inbuilt editor, editing with Picasa, editing using MS Word and power point. These are extremely simple to understand but one can do a lot of alterations like colour correction rest exposure correction composition correction change. All these editing are explained with flower pictures.

Flower photography is very appealing and very easy to learn. But some basics of photography is required. It is discussed in detail in my own book " learning photography made easy" available in Amazon. But here, I have discussed the important aspects from that book, with respect to flower photography

Basic controls in a camera.

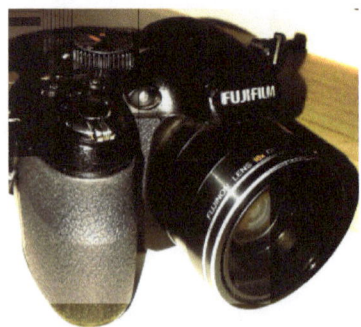

Flower Photography

There are six basic variables that are to be understood and controlled. They are:
1. Aperture
2. Shutter speed
3. Depth of field
4. Colour temperature
5. P, A, S and M modes.
6. ISO setting

1] Aperture:

It is the opening of the centre portion of the lens to control the light falling on to the film or CCD screen.

The basic rule of the aperture is:-
The Larger the aperture, more the light.

Aperture is used for controlling amount of light entering through the lens of the camera.

- It is made up of very thin metal leaf segments overlapping on one another.

- When we rotate the control, the leaf opening varies, allowing more or less light.

Wide open aperture allows maximum light and small opening allows less or minimum light. *But the aperture size will not be measured in millimetre.*

It is not the diameter, but a parameter called

"f number"

"f number" = diameter of the opening/ focal length.

3

Jayaram as

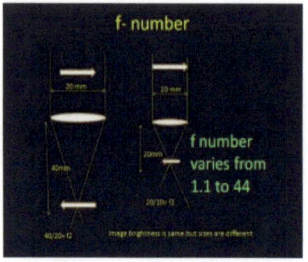

"f number" normally varies from 2.8 to 22, 2.8 being maximum opening and 22 being minimum opening. Of course, in some high end cameras, f number starts from 1.2 to 44. But most of the situations can be managed from f number 2.8 to 22. Also, high end cameras are costly.

Note:-

As f number increases, aperture opening decreases, and hence the light entering through the lens decreases, if the time is kept same.

The following figures will make the concept clear.

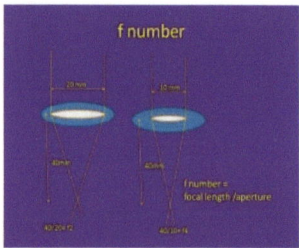

In the above figure, focal length of the lens is 40mm and the diameter of the opening is 20mm in first case. So, f number is 40/20=2. This is called setting aperture to f2.

In second case in the same figure, same lens of 40mm focal length but opening is only 10mm. So, f number is given by 40/10 =4. This is called setting aperture to f4.

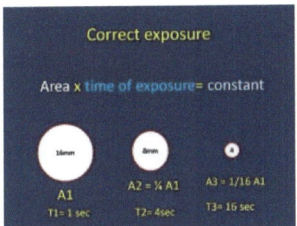

2] Shutter speed or time of exposure.

If the aperture is smaller, we have to give more *time* for get correct exposure. That means:

The total light = area of the aperture X time of exposure.

This concept is illustrated by the previous figure and next figure.

Area of the aperture X time of exposure = should be constant (for a particular ISO setting, which is discussed in point number 5 of this section.)

Time of exposure.

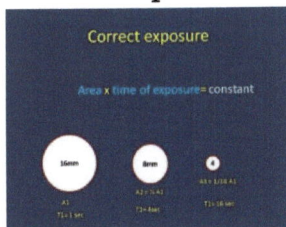

By looking at the previous two figures, it is very clear that for a particular situation, ***there will be many correct exposures!***

Let us consider to cases.

- We can give a correct exposure for area A1 and time t1

OR

- We can Double the area and expose for ½ of the time

OR

- If we reduce the area to $1/4^{th}$ then we have to give the exposure time 4 times.

All these combinations give correct exposures! Then which one should we select and why?

For this, we have to understand what is called

"Depth of field"

3] Depth of field.

We will see Three dimensions in real life, because we are having two eyes! But the camera is having only one lens and so, it gives only two dimensions. (3D cameras with 2 lenses are already arriving)

But we can make a viewer to have a feel of three dimensions by controlling the third dimension of depth of field. So, now let us try to understand the concept of 'depth of field' in a photograph.

Let us consider a photograph.

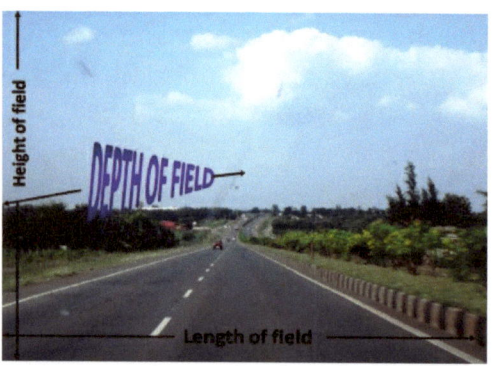

The distance from your left end to right end in frame of the photo is called of the 'length of field'.

The distance from your top most point to bottom most point in the frame of the photo is called 'height if field'.

Everything from the camera lens to the front most horizons that you can capture in the frame is called as 'depth of field'.

But in photography, that distance up to which objects are fairly clear and not blur is called as 'depth of field'

Note:- A lens can be focussed to only one object at a time. So, getting all the things in focus is not possible. But by adjusting the aperture size, we can get the desired depth of field. That is illustrated by the following photos.

Flower Photography

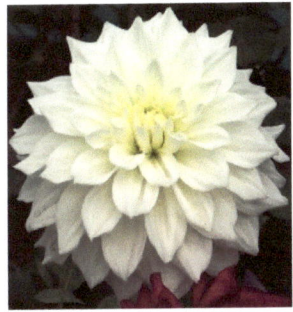

Large aperture gives small depth of field.
It is the most important but most neglected subject of photography. Even though the new digital cameras can almost take pictures on any subject in any conditions, it cannot take picture "as you want". This is because in the same frame or composition, you may focus an object of your interest only, making other thing in the background blur, by adjusting the aperture suitably.
As an illustration, in the photo of a flower above, with aperture kept wide open, say f4, to intentionally blur the background. If the aperture is closed more, depth of field is increased, so that ugly back ground will also be in focus. Of course, one should have a digital camera with manual mode to adjust the aperture, to get the above results.

Large depth of view gives all in focus!

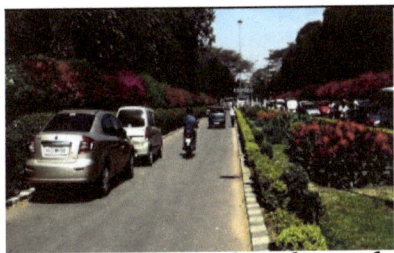

Small aperture gives large depth of field
Let us look at another photo in which aperture is kept small, so as to increase the depth of field. Here, from the nearest object to the farthest object are in focus.
Even though the new digital cameras can almost take pictures on any subject in any conditions, it cannot take picture "as you want". This is because in the same frame or composition, you may focus an object of your interest only, making other thing in the background blur, by adjusting the aperture suitably.

So, whatever may be the advancement of the camera technology, it cannot understand your intention many times. That is why, in many cameras, different modes like close up, beach, indoor ... will be provided. But it cannot substitute your intelligence and creativity.

    4] colour temperature.

Every camera will have a basic adjustment for colour temperature correction. Most neglected concept is that the 'correct colour of the photo depends also on the colour of the light falling on the object'.

Colour temperature of tube light is different from that of a bulb light and so on. So, we have to first adjust the camera for this. Go to manual mode. Then in settings, select 'white balance'. The following modes are available.

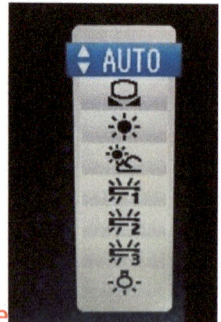

Auto mode

Flower Photography

The adjustment menu is called "white Balance".

Look at the photo; it is directly taken from the display screen of a digital camera.

When you cannot decide the correct colour due to combination of light etc, then you have to select 'Auto' mode. The camera decides the correct colour to the possible extent.

Custom mode

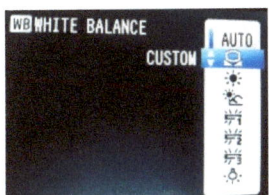 'custom' mode is used to take lots of photos in a fixed type of lighting, say bulb. This allows you to adjust the colour to your liking and set it as custom. Even in tricky situations, you can adjust all settings and make it as custom.

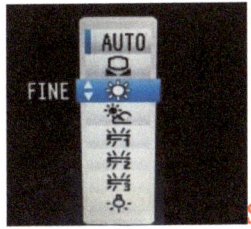 ### Sun light mode

This is the symbol for sunlight mode. It is normally used for all day light photos. But, note that sun light colour is correct to this mode from 10AM to 4PM. You know that early morning and in the evening, sun light will be reddish in colour.

Shade mode

This is the symbol for shady sunlight area. The requirement of this is use full mainly when it is a cloudy day. A bad weather is good day for certain type of photography where even lighting is required. This mode is also use full for partially sunlight areas.

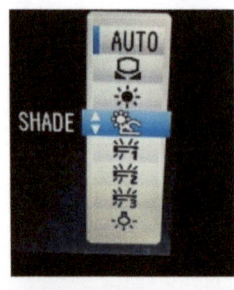Artificial light modes

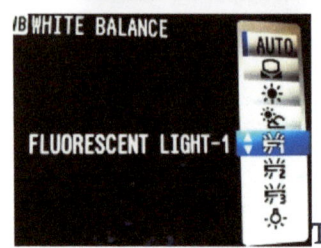The three symbols are for tube lights. The first is for normal tube light of 1mt length.

The second one is for 50 cm emergency tube light.

The third one is for CFL type tube. If your camera is having only one tube light setting, do not worry. All the above three tubes are almost the same colour temperature.

Bulb mode

Flower Photography

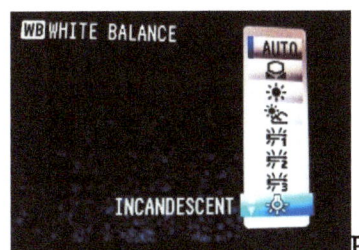
Fourth one is for the bulb light. It is also called incandescent light or filament light. It is having yellowish temperature. So if you take photos in tube mode with bulb light you will find large colour error.

Now, try all above things and even with wrong adjustments and learn the effect of colour temperature. Take some pictures in tube light by adjusting to bulb mode and analyse the colour errors. Sometimes, Wrong settings are used to get special effects in 'trick photography'.

P, A, S and M modes.

The photo below illustrates different shooting modes like P, A, S, and M.

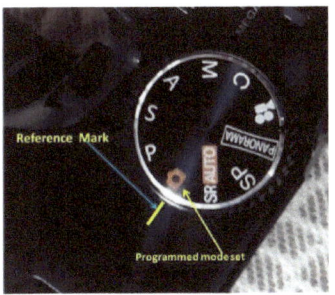

The above photo shows the dial of the camera set to 'programmed

Jayaram as mode'.

P mode is programmed mode:

In this mode,

* The camera selects the best shutter and aperture depending on the light and other conditions.
* We can program this and store this in some cameras.
*it is mainly for taking many different photos under similar conditions.

S mode : Shutter priority mode

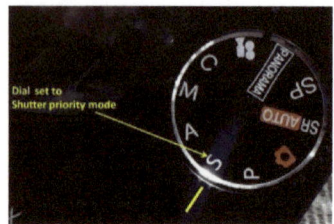

S mode :

It is shutter priority mode. Shutter opening and closing time can be controlled in this mode:

*camera will control aperture, to give correct exposure

*normally from a maximum of 8 sec to 1/2000 sec can be varied in steps.

* Long exposures (> 1/30 sec) are used only when the camera is on a tripod stand, else there will be camera shake because of our hand vibration.

*normal exposures (1/60 to 1/250 sec) are used for all out door shootings on a bright sunny day

* high speeds (< 1/250 sec to 1/2000 sec) are used for sports, etc.

A mode: Aperture priority mode.

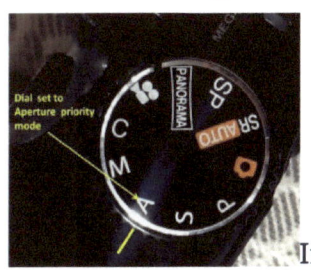In this mode, the opening of the aperture can be controlled.

* Aperture is varied to control the light and/or *depth of field.*

*camera will control shutter, to give correct exposure.

M mode : Manual mode.

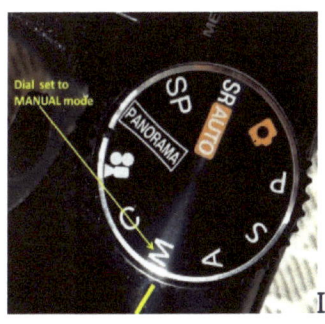In this mode, everything can be controlled.

*creativity starts here, as we can make any type of control.

* We have full control over shutter speed as well as aperture.

* for all other modes, exposure will be correct, but in this mode we can make a bright day as a dim lit day etc.

These modifications by breaking the rules are to give special effects.

The display screen indicates the mode that is set. Here it is indicating Manual mode.

It also indicates the controls that you can do in each mode. Of course, this indication will obstruct the view of the image in the screen. So, it will be indicated for only about 5 seconds. Afterwards, screen will be seen as a clear view finder, displaying the frame of the image that we are going to capture.

The display of the controls and variables will be switched 'on' or 'off', as and when required, by a separate button in the camera.

Different control display is illustrated in the next photo below.

Look at the above photo of the display of camera screen, when Manual mode is set.

Left end of the screen is showing 'shutter speed'. In this case, it is set at 1/100 seconds.

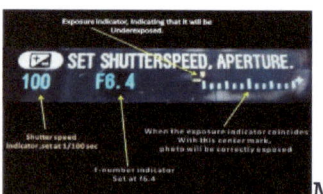Middle portion of the screen indicates f number. In this case, it is set at F6.4.

Right side of the screen displays exposure indicator.

If the reference mark is exactly at the centre, we will get the correct exposure.

If the reference mark is to the left side of the centre mark (that is toward negative sign), then we will get under exposure.

If the reference mark is to the right side of the centre mark (that is toward positive sign), then we will get over exposure.

So, we should adjust controls to see that the exposure indicator coincides exactly to the centre mark, to get correct exposure.

Suppose, we require f number to be f8. Then set the f number to f8. Vary the shutter speed and make the exposure indicator to coincide with the centre of the reference mark.

Similarly, suppose, we require shutter speed to be 1/250 seconds. Then set shutter speed to 1/125sec. Vary the f number and make the exposure indicator to almost coincide with the centre of the reference mark.

If there is a small difference between the centre of the reference mark and the exposure indicator, do not worry. It will not affect the exposure to noticeable extent. In fact, many times you cannot make it to coincide exactly, as both f number and shutter speed vary in steps and not continuously.

6] ISO setting

This is a tricky parameter. It is the International Standard Organization which has standardized the film speed or sensitivity.

In digital camera, there will not be any film to store the image; it is captured by Charge Coupled Device, known as CCD in short. The area of the CCD and its fineness is responsible for Pixel of the camera. As we know, higher the megapixel, more the resolution of the captured image. Also, the sensitivity to light also depends upon the area of the CCD and to some extent, the associated electronic circuit.

For every camera, there will be a base ISO. Say, for my camera, it is 100 ISO. So, at 100 ISO setting, it captures the rated megapixel, in my camera it is 18 megapixels.

Now, let us try to understand the effect of varying ISO.

For 100 ISO, if the correct exposure requires a shutter speed of 1/100 seconds for F3.1, then

For 200 ISO, it will be 1/200seconds; for same F3.1

For 400 ISO, it will be 1/400 seconds; for same F3.1

and so on. That means,

The product of ISO and Time = constant for a particular f- number. Therefore, increasing ISO means Increasing sensitivity .When the ISO is increased, the time of

exposure will decrease proportionately. So, the vibration of the camera at low speeds can be avoided by increasing ISO and exposing at high speed.

Look at the following Pictures.

The first one, marked as A, is exposed at 100 ISO and the time of exposure is

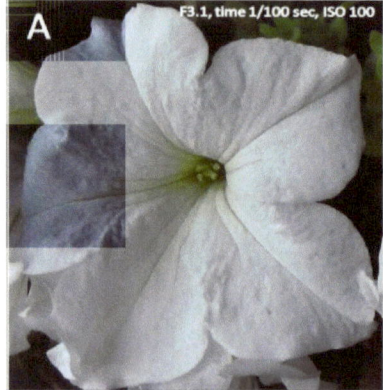

1/100th of a second. Observe the noise. It is hardly

visible.
Look at the next photo marked as B
It is exposed at 200 ISO and hence the time of exposure is 1/200th of a second.

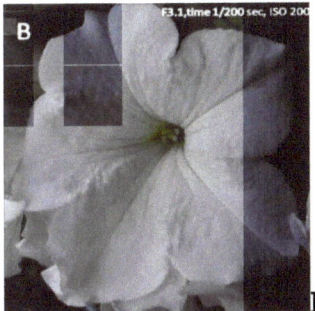

In this photo, the grains are slightly visible.

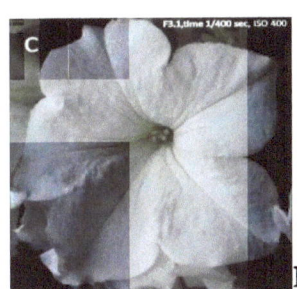

Look at the next photo, marked as C. It is

exposed at

400 ISO and hence the time of exposure is 1/400th of a second. In this photo, grains are clearly visible.
Look at the next photo marked as D.

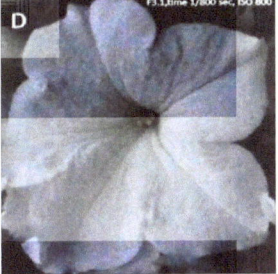

It is exposed at 800 ISO and hence the time of exposure is 1/800th of a second. This Picture is full of grains.
So, when we want to enlarge a picture for large size
Printing, grains or noise really matters but when it is only for sharing in the web or to view only in mobile or laptop we can

17

tolerate little grains.

You will learn more in the following illustrative examples.

Illustrative examples.

First, let us consider an example of a flower photo, in which f-number is kept constant but shutter speed is varied.

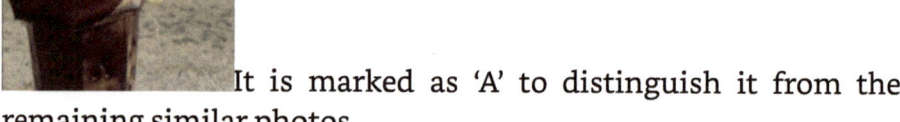It is marked as 'A' to distinguish it from the remaining similar photos.

As we can see, this is a case of 'over exposure'. In photography, we say that most of the details are 'washed out'.

Here, f number is 6.4 and the shutter speed is 1/200 second.

The flower is kept in door, but since the door is open, it is actually having Sun light.

The back ground is also visible. For the remaining photos, the same location is used with same intensity of Sun light. Only the shutter speed will be different.

This is marked as 'B'.

Flower Photography

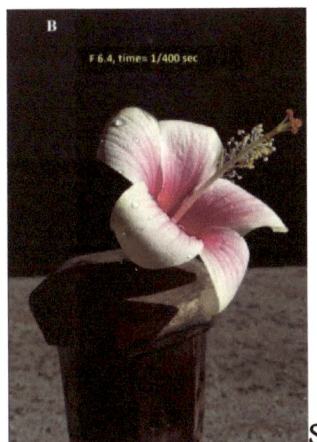

Same f 6.4 but shutter speed is 1/400 second. It means, the light is ½ of the previous photo.

This is 'correct exposure', as read from the camera meter.

Here, almost all the details are visible. Look at the small droplets on petals of the flower. They are shining from the Sun light, falling from an angle.

The back ground is slightly visible.

This is marked as 'c'.

Here also, f- number is same as f6.4, but shutter speed is 1/1000 seconds.

Compared to 'A', the light is $1/5^{th}$ only. This is considered as 'under exposure', according to camera meter.

But still the droplet is shining and also, the petal that is nearer to us seems to be correctly exposed!

Introduction to flower photography.

Flower is the most appealing thing in photography, after face. Its colours, designs, sizes, shapes and arrangements are fascinating. Even though flowers are not having feelings and expressions visibly, these can inspire us at all times. In this book, I will try to explain simple ways of getting good photographs of flowers.

Parameters that are to be considered while taking flower photograph

are

- Light
- Direction of light and Camera angle in front of the flower
- Back ground and framing
- Type and size of the flower to be selected
- Flower arrangements
- Flower shows

Light

Here, we can select

Sunlight or day light: *it is the most advantageous light. Many times, direct sunlight will not be appealing.*

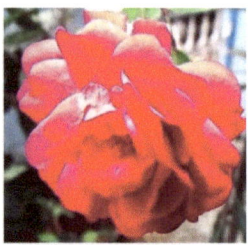

Top lighting – Sun light

A cloudy day is very good, as diffused light will be there. Also, we can keep the flower with pot, in shade.

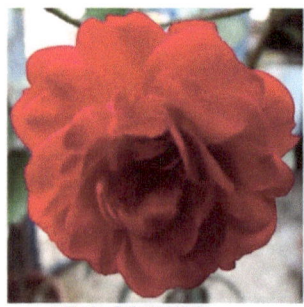

Cloudy – Diffused LIGHT

Flash light: *it should be used to take photos at night, with dark sky back ground.*

Bulb light: *Normally used to get the effect of side lighting during the night.*

Combination: *when the flower is large or to get fill in effect, a combination of day light with flash is to be used.*

- *Direction of light and Camera angle in front of the flower*
The direction of light is very important in flower photography.

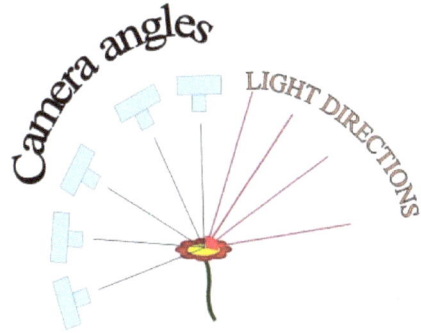

Above photo illustrate the concept. About 5 camera angles and about 4 light directions will make a combination of 20 photos that you have to take, to understand the effect.

The photos bellow illustrates it

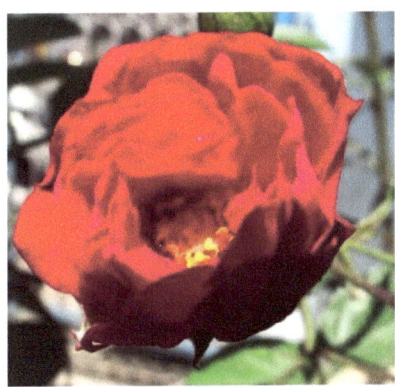

A good combination of camera angle and light
To get a part of pollen illuminated by sun light

This article emphasizes 5 important tips for getting good photos of flowers.

1] Selecting the right kind of flower

There are many appealing flowers like rose, dahlia, and hibiscus and so on. Depending upon the season, we can select the kind of flower that we have to photograph. The colour and size of the flower are then decided and many photographs are to be taken with many colours and sizes of flowers.

2] Camera angle and direction of light

The camera angle with respect to the flower is a very important one. It is actually a combination of light camera and flower angle. So, while considering the camera angle, we have to consider direction at which light is falling on to the flower. In general, light should fall at 45^0 with respect to the imaginary line joining flower to the camera. Sun light is best compared to artificial lighting.

3] Back ground

Plain back ground is best for flower photography. Normally, clear sky will be the best. If the sky background is not possible and the existing background is distracting, it can be blurred by controlling the depth of field

4] Depth of field and aperture

It is the tolerable focus of the background behind the subject. As the aperture size increases, depth of field decreases and it will be blurred but the flower will be in focus. So, in such cases, aperture should be F4, where f number is the measurement of aperture.

5] Shutter speed

To reduce the effect of hand vibrations while taking photograph, a fast shutter speed is required, but it should be selected in combination of aperture and light intensity. Normally, 1/125 or 1/500 second is used when wind is making the flower to move.

With respect to taking photographs, flowers are mainly classified as

- Small flowers
- Medium sized flowers
- Large flowers.

The methodology of taking photo varies depending upon the size of flowers.

Small flowers.

Small flowers are arranged in large groups. These are used for borders of lawn and such other places.

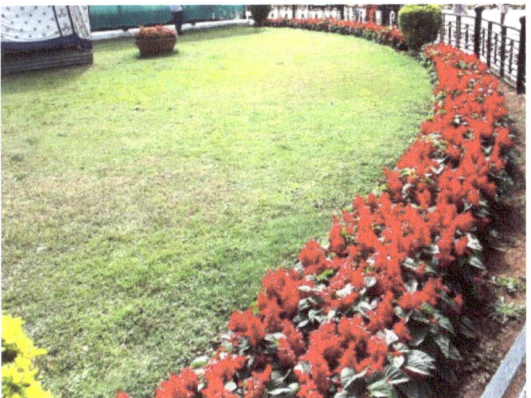

Some small flowers are arranged in the big pot. We can have many colored flowers in one pot.

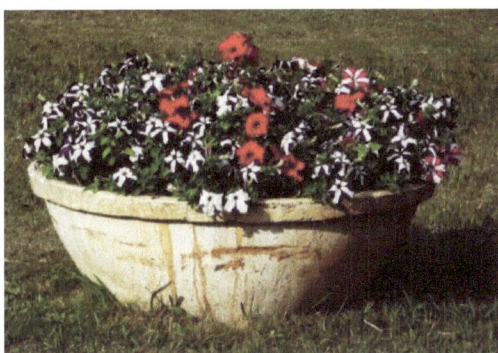

These can also be placed by grouping many number of pots put together. This method is having advantage of altering the arrangement by re arranging the pots.

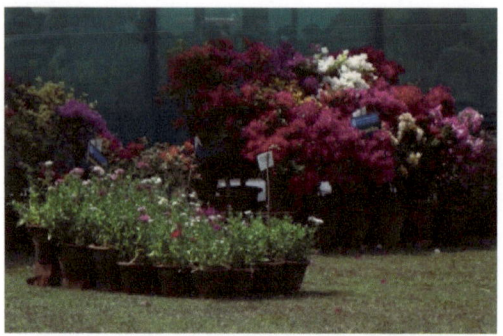

Taking photograph after arranging them in a particular order as shown below will be very attractive. The camera light metering should be set to "average" position.

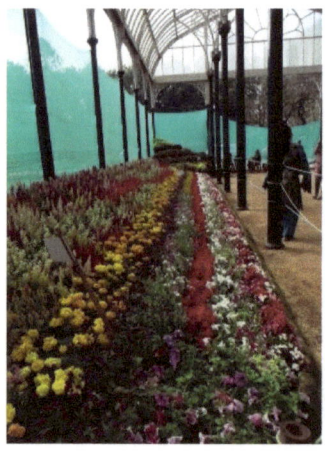

Very small flowers can be in only one pot, as shown to add beauty . This can be photographed at different angles.

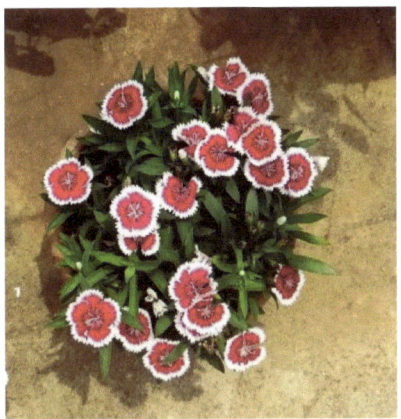

Tiny flowers are suitable for close up photos. Aperture should be wide open to reduce the depth of field so that the back ground is blurred, giving more emphasis to the flowers.

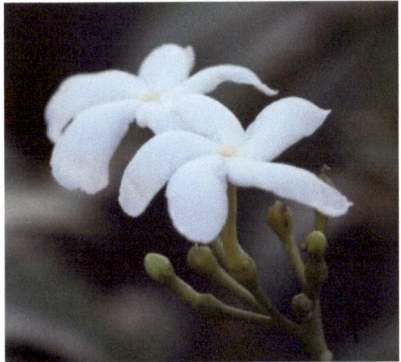

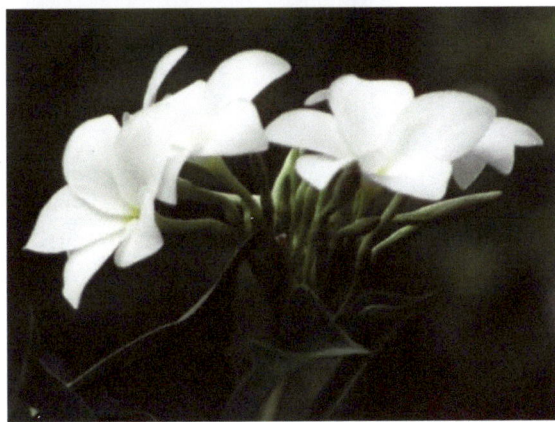

Medium sized flowers.

These are the actual materials that will make up 80% of flower photography. Most of the prizes in flower photography are from this sector. This is because roses are in this category. But as you go through the book, ypu will realize that many other flowers in medium size are equally beautiful.

Since it it very important to select required settings in the camera, i have explained each flower photo here in terms of camera settings and other parameters like general, back ground, direction of lighting, camera angle, exposure and composition.

Flower-1

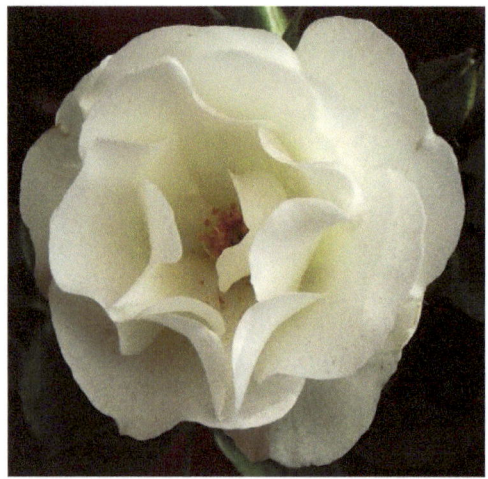

General :

This is not rose. White petals are indicating how tender they are. Petals are straight, lights and shadows are not enhanced.

Background :

Green leafy back ground is ideal because of white colour of the flower. The back ground can also be changed during editing but initial selection of black back ground is preferred.

Direction of lighting :

Lighting should be at an angle, preferably from top downwards.

Camera angle :

It is easy in this picture. Details of petals are seen.

Exposure :

Exposure is as usual to any other flower. This aspect can be easily edited and so, we need not have to worry too much about this. But a very wrong exposure cannot be completely corrected.

Composition :

For all these medium sized flowers shown as single flower, tight composition is done. That is, only flower and no extra back ground is shown.

Flower-2

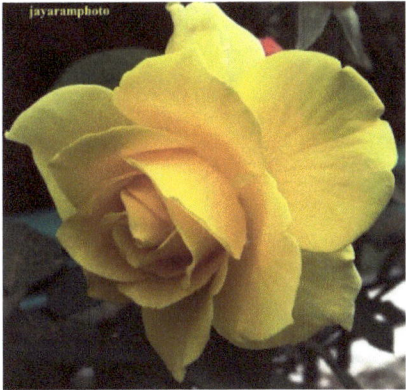

General :

This yellow rose is a beautiful flower. Petals are not curling and so it is easy to get a good angle for this picture. Since it is inclined, innermost petals are not visible, but still it is beautiful.

Background :

It is partly leafy but partly white as it was available at that place. We can change it to black but the present back ground looks natural.

Direction of lighting :

Lighting is from the sky to downwards, as it was at 12 noon.

Camera angle :

It is selected here to see the details of outer petals.

Exposure :

Exposure is as usual to any other flower.

Composition :

For all these medium sized flowers shown as single flower, tight composition is done. That is, only flower and no extra back ground is shown.

Flower-3

Flower Photography

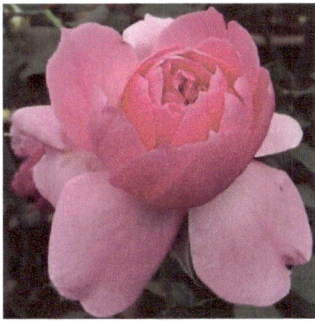

General :

This is pink rose. We can observe the details in each petal, which is enhancing for the beauty of the picture.

Background :

Green leafy back ground is ideal because of white colour of the flower

Direction of lighting :

Top to downwards.

Camera angle :

Since the flower is facing upwards, horizontal direction of the camera is selected.

Exposure :

Exposure is as usual to any other flower.

Composition :

For all these medium sized flowers shown as single flower, tight composition is done. That is, only flower and no extra back ground is shown.

Flower-4

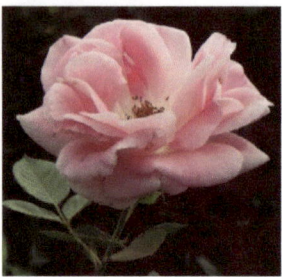

General :

This is not rose. Inner petal gap is wide and pollens are visible. Petals are thick and little curly.

Background :

Black back ground is ideal because of white colour of the flower. The nearest two or three leaves which are focused added beauty to the flower.

Direction of lighting :

Top to downwards.

Camera angle :

Since the flower is facing upwards, horizontal direction of the camera is selected. But since it is digital world, we can take several pictures at different camera angles and the best one can be selected.

Exposure :

Exposure is as usual to any other flower.

Composition :

Flower Photography

For all these medium sized flowers shown as single flower, tight composition is done. That is, only flower and no extra back ground is shown.

Flower-5

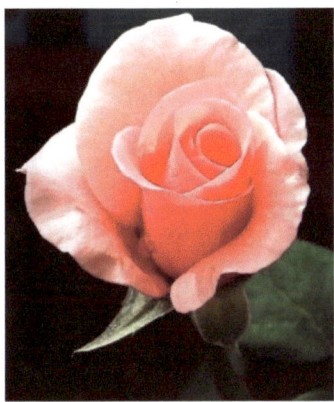

General :

This is the gem of flowers. Rose colored petals are indicating how tender they are. Petals are curling outwards and upwards, adding beauty to flower.

Background :

Black back ground is ideal because of rose colour of the flower. The nearest two or three leaves which are focused added beauty to the flower.

Direction of lighting :

Top to downwards.

Camera angle :

Since the flower is facing upwards, horizontal direction of the camera is selected.

Exposure :

As usual.

Composition :

Tight composition is done.

Flower-6

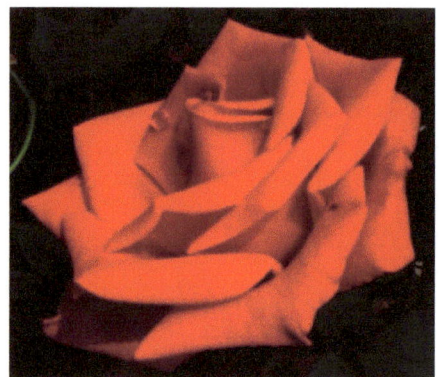

General :

Words cannot explain the beauty of this flower! Just see the picture and enjoy it. Red rose is the most famous flower among roses. Petals are curling too much and lights and shadows are enhanced.

Background :

Black back ground is ideal because of red colour of the flower. The back ground has been edited to make it perfectly black.

Direction of lighting :

Flower is facing upwards and Sunlight is from top to downwards.

Camera angle :

Perfectly horizontal direction of the camera is selected. Some of the outer petals are obscuring the inner petals but it is adding to the beauty of the picture.

Exposure :

Exposure is as usual to any other flower.

Composition :

For all these medium sized flowers shown as single flower, tight composition is done. That is, only flower and no extra back ground is shown.

Flower-7

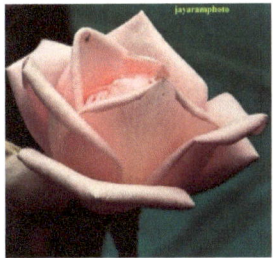

General :

This is a beautiful rose flower. The petals are indicating how tender they are. Petals are curling outwards and so, lights and shadows are enhanced. A slight variation of exposure will spoil the beauty of this picture. We can observe the details in each petal, which is enhancing for the beauty of the picture.

Background :

Light green back ground is ideal because of rose colour of the flower. The back ground can also be changed during editing but initial selection of black back ground is preferred.

Direction of lighting :

Lighting should be at an angle, preferably from right or left side to downwards at 45 degrees inclination as shown in the picture.

Camera angle :

Horizontal angle of the camera is selected. But since it is digital world, we can take several pictures at different camera angles and the best one can be selected.

Exposure :

Exposure is as usual to any other flower. This aspect can be easily edited and so, we need not have to worry too much about this. But a very wrong exposure cannot be completely corrected.

Composition :

For all these medium sized flowers shown as single flower, tight composition is done. That is, only flower and no extra back ground is shown.

Flower-8

Flower Photography

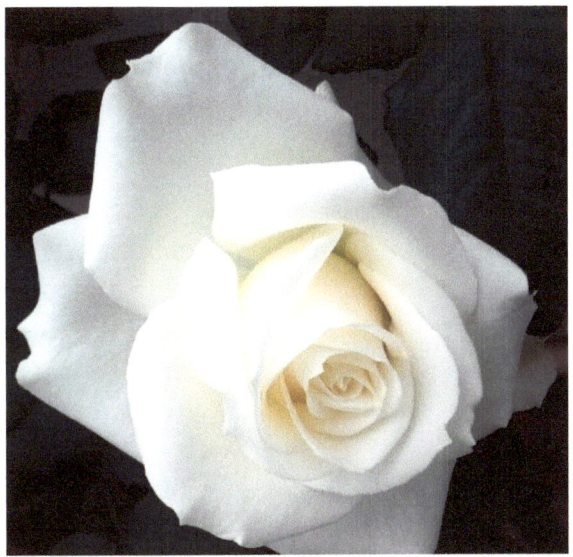

General :

This is the gem of flowers. White rose petals are indicating how tender they are. Petals are curling outwards and so, lights and shadows are enhanced. A slight variation of exposure will spoil the beauty of this picture. We can observe the details in each petal, which is enhancing for the beauty of the picture.

Note : normally, it is very difficult to get a flower without any error in petals. Many a times, some black patches, small holes or some such thing will be there. So, before selecting the flower for photographing, we have to examine the flower carefully.

Background :

Black back ground is ideal because of white colour of the flower. The back ground can also be changed during editing but initial selection of black back ground is preferred.

Direction of lighting:

This is actually extremely important. Lighting should be at an angle, preferably from left or right side to downwards at 45 degrees inclination as shown in the picture.

Camera angle:

It is selected in such a way that the picture contains details of inner most petal to outermost petal. If the camera angle is changed a little, some of the outer petals will obscure the inner petals and spoils the beauty of the picture. Here , almost the horizontal position of the camera is selected.

Exposure :

Exposure is as usual to any other flower. This aspect can be easily edited and so, we need not have to worry too much about this. Since it is extremely beautiful and tender, many variations of exposure may be explored and the best one is selected.

Composition :

For all these medium sized flowers shown as single flower, tight composition is done. That is, only flower and no extra back ground is shown.

Flower-9

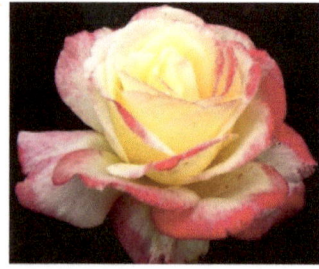

General :

This is rose with double colored petals. We can observe the

details in each petal, which is enhancing for the beauty of the picture. The color streams of red in flowers are adding to the beauty of the flower.

Background :

Black back ground is ideal because of white and red colour of the flower. The back ground can also be changed during editing but initial selection of black back ground is preferred.

Direction of lighting :

It is from top to downwards, almost directly below the Sun.

Camera angle :

Horizontal position of the camera is selected, as for most of the flowers.

Exposure :

Exposure is as usual to any other flower. This aspect can be easily edited and so, we need not have to worry too much about this. But a very wrong exposure cannot be completely corrected.

Composition :

For all these medium sized flowers shown as single flower, tight composition is done. That is, only flower and no extra back ground is shown.

Flower-10

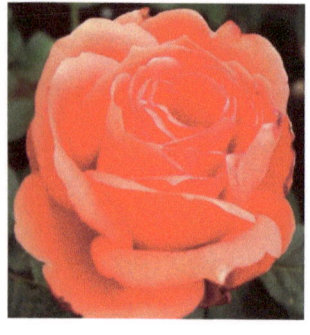

General :

This is rose with red colored petals. The petals are quite thick, not allowing much of the light to pass through. So, it is almost looking like a painted picture.

Background :

Green back ground is ideal because of red colour of the flower. The back ground can also be changed during editing but initial selection of black back ground is preferred.

Direction of lighting :

Lighting should be at an angle, preferably from left or right side to downwards at 45 degrees inclination as shown in the picture.

Camera angle :

Flower is almost vertical and so, horizontal camara position is selected.

Exposure :

Exposure is as usual to any other flower. This aspect can be easily edited and so, we need not have to worry too much about this. But a very wrong exposure cannot be completely corrected.

Composition :

For all these medium sized flowers shown as single flower,

tight composition is done. That is, only flower and no extra back ground is shown.

Flower-11

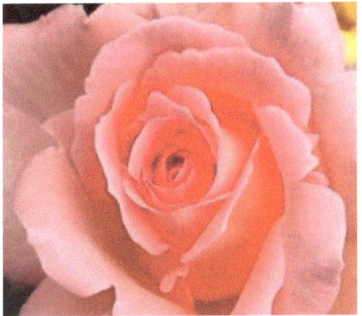

General :

This is close up picture of a rose flower with rose petals. Many inner petal circles are adding to the beauty of the flower.

Background :

There is no other back ground is existing in this picture! The flower itself with petals is making the back ground.

Direction of lighting :

Lighting should be at an angle, preferably from left or right side to downwards at 45 degrees inclination as shown in the picture.

Camera angle :

It is selected in such a way that the picture contains details of inner most petal to outermost petal. Flower is slightly inclined and the camera angle is adjusted to get the maximum details.

Exposure :

Exposure is as usual to any other flower. This aspect can be easily edited and so, we need not have to worry too much about this. But a very wrong exposure cannot be completely corrected.

Composition :

For all these medium sized flowers shown as single flower, tight composition is done. That is, only flower and no extra back ground is shown.

Large flowers: Hibiscus flower

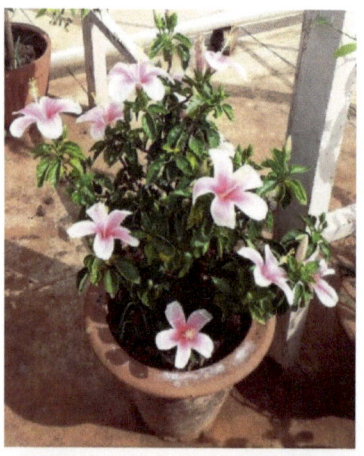

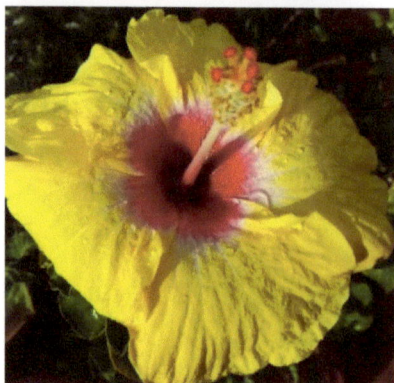

General:

This is a large size flower. Most of these are captured as only one flower but, we can capture them in groups also, as shown in the previous photograph.

Sprinkling of water on hibiscus flower is normally done as it is a big flower. With the side lighting and suitable camera angle we can see the shining of many of the droplets, which is extremely appealing. It can be seen in the above photo.

Background:

Black back ground is ideal because of white colour of the flower. The back ground can also be changed during editing but initial selection of black back ground is preferred.

Direction of lighting :

Lighting should be at an angle, preferably from left or right side to downwards at 45 degrees inclination as shown in the picture.

Camera angle :

it is selected in such a way that the picture contains details of inner most petal to outermost petal.

Exposure:

Exposure is as usual to any other flower. This aspect can be easily edited and so, we need not have to worry too much about this. But a very wrong exposure cannot be completely corrected.

Composition :

For all these medium sized flowers shown as single flower, tight composition is done. That is, only flower and no extra back ground is shown.

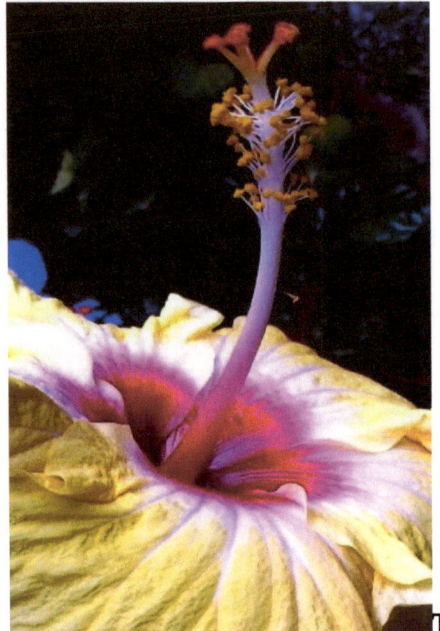

The hibiscus flower is having well exposed pollen grains this is a very appealing thing and taking photograph of pollen grains with extreme close up is one of the highlight of hibiscus photography. But when we are at the extreme close up, the depth of field will be less. So when we focus on the pollen grains normally the petals of the hibiscus flower will be out of focus. If you want both of them to be in focus, the F number should be more and a bright sunlight is required. If the light is very low, it is very difficult to achieve this kind of a thing.

When showing pollen grains, direction of light is extremely important. In some cases as shown below, we can even have the shadow of the pollen grains falling and one of the petals to enhance the beauty of the photograph. But in such case the direction of lighting and the camera angle are extremely important.

Flower Photography

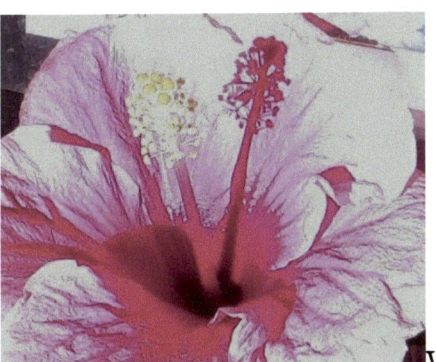
We can clearly see the shadow of the pollen on the petal, which is more prominent than the actual pollen itself.

Dahlia flower.

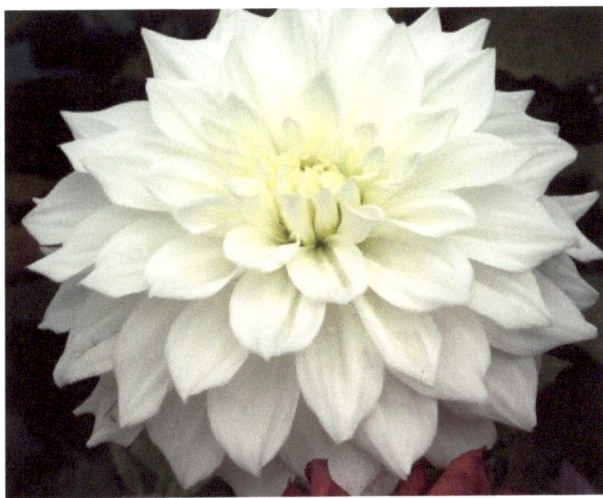

General:
This is also one of the large size flowers. Some flowers many times larger than hibiscus. The large flower size can be comparable with sunflower. One of the highlight of this flower is the curling of

many petals in circles, giving lot of shades and extremely good photograph. Also it is available in many colors, even though pink and white are extremely popular. Some people will be taking pictures of yellow colour flowers. One of the white color flower shown here is extremely appealing.

Camera angle:

Notice that these flowers will always be facing horizontal and not upwards. Therefore the camera angle is horizontal many times showing face of the flower or at an angle to the face of the flower.

Light must be from the opposite angle so that we can get the grey shades within the petals excellently.

Background:

In most of the cases only one flower will be in a frame with a tight background. Dark background sometimes a single day live flower will be shot with the dark blue sky as the background but in that case the angle of the sunlight the flower and the camera positions are extremely important.

```
Camera Model: FinePix S1800
Equipment Make: FUJIFILM
Date Taken: 22-01-2012 11:02:53
Color Representation: sRGB
Subject Distance:
Flash Used: No
Focal Length: 33 mm
F-Number: F/5.3
Exposure Time: 1/210 sec.
Metering Mode: Pattern
Exposure Compensation: 0 step
```

Exposure:

Complete information of the camera settings are given above. After the initial information about the camera model and date, notice that

- RGB is the color system called Red, Blue and Green.
- Distance information not shown
- Flash – not used
- Focal length = 33mm (read basics as explained

initially)
- F number= 5.3
- Exposure time =1/210.
- Light metering =pattern = average.

Multi colored flowers:

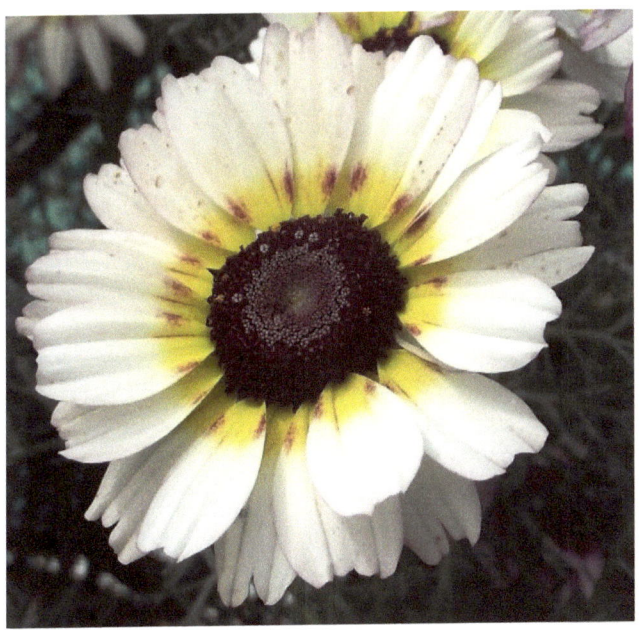

General :

Nature is the best painter! Look at the flower above. It is more than painting. Symmetry of nature is superb. It is all to attract a butterfly for pollination. Even though it is a small flower, lots of details are here.

Background :

Black back ground is ideal because of white colour of the flower. The back ground can also be changed during editing but initial selection of black back ground is preferred.

Direction of lighting :

Lighting is from top from direct Sunlight.

Camera angle :

For this flower having almost single layer of petals, a 45 degree angle with respect to the flower is selected.

Exposure :

Exposure is as usual to any other flower. This aspect can be easily edited and so, we need not have to worry too much about this. But a very wrong exposure cannot be completely corrected.

Composition :

For all these medium sized flowers shown as single flower, tight composition is done. That is, only flower and no extra back ground is shown.

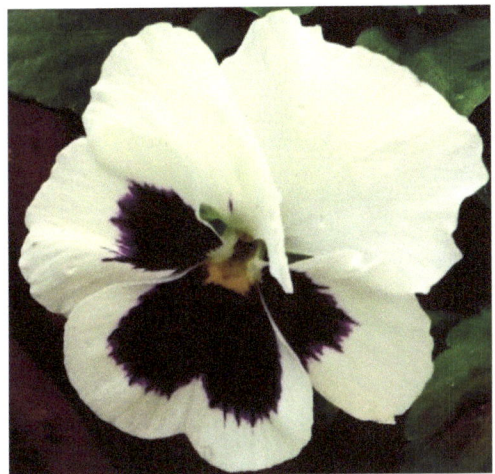

This is a magic. It looks as if you have painted some of the petals of a white flower!

Exposure and all other things are same as before.

May flower or thunder flower!

The flower shown below is a very large collection of small flowers, giving us a feeling that it is a single large flower. It blooms only in the month of May in India, during the starting of the monsoon with thunder storms. Hence the name of the flower is May flower or thunder flower

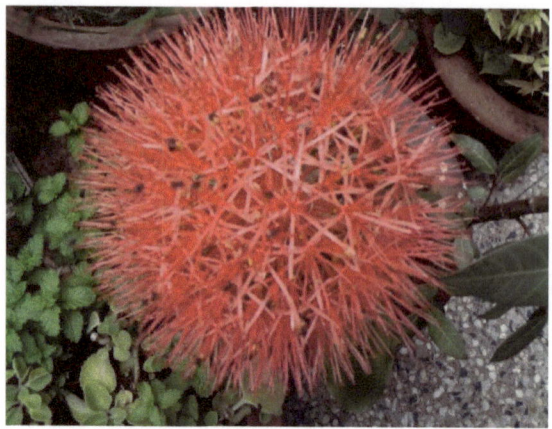

Any lighting with any camera angle will do for this because of its perfect spherical shape! It can be seen only for a month in the whole of the year.

Flowers with insects or butterfly:

Most of the flower photos are having a butterfly sitting on it to make it lively!

We cannot think of adjusting all the settings of the camera, as the insect will give us an opportunity for a few seconds. So, auto mode is proffered and any corrections required for the exposure are to be done during editing.

Photo below shows a bee sitting on the flower.

Flower Photography

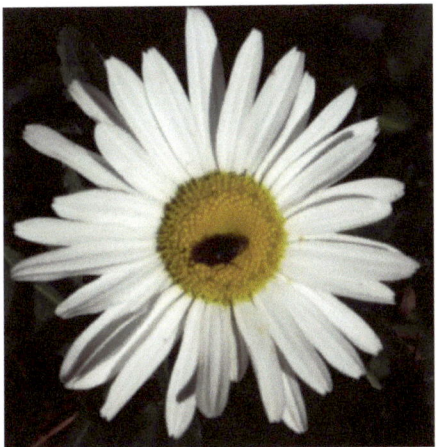

Even a small ant in the flower can make it lively, as shown in the flower below.

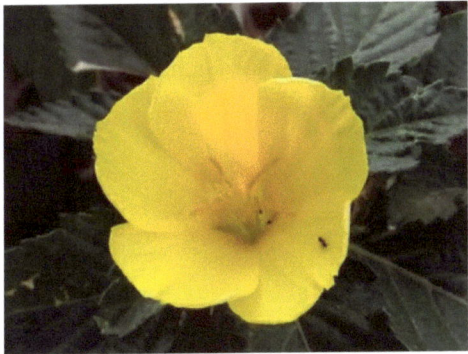

Editing:

In this digital era, most of the photographs are edited. No photograph is 100% perfect. So, some editing is required. Also, we can add text, back ground and so on for almost perfect photo, during editing.

I have give editing using free software which is almost inbuilt in windows. So, no question of purchasing any software.

One of the most important in built photo editing toll is "Microsoft office picture manager". So, initially that method has been explained.

Steps:

- Click on the picture you want to edit.
- Select "open with" option.
- In that option, select "Microsoft office picture manager"
- Then the picture will open as shown.
- Click " edit picture" at the top.
- Select " brightness and contrast settings"

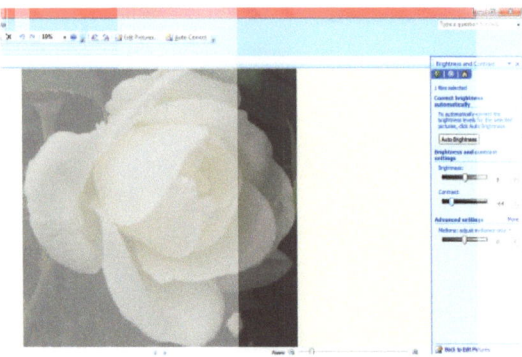

The above rose is made soft looking by reducing contrast to a very low value.

Lengthy are not required description for these things. One can easily practice and learn.

The contrast is increased to a maximum in the photo below. It resulted in harsh shades. Both these extremes are not appealing.

Flower Photography

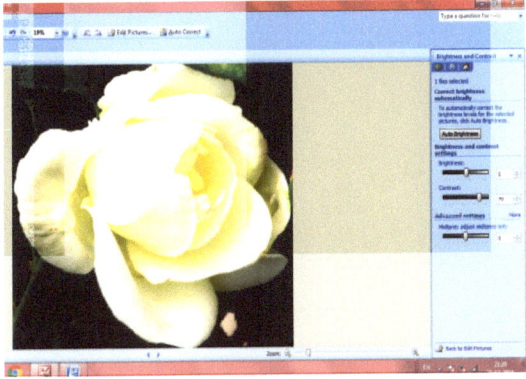

Almost god balance is achieved in the photo below.

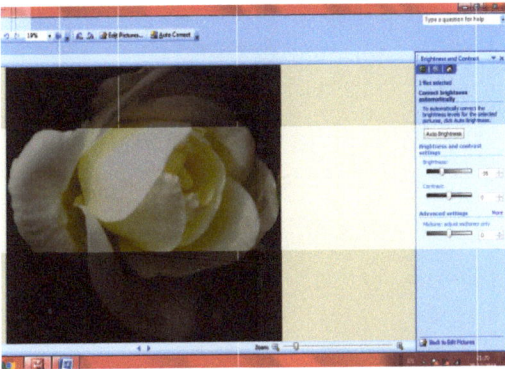

Another parameter called mid tone adjusement is also seen here. When the mid tones are very low, complete dark back ground is achived as shown below. Shades are varying in good way.

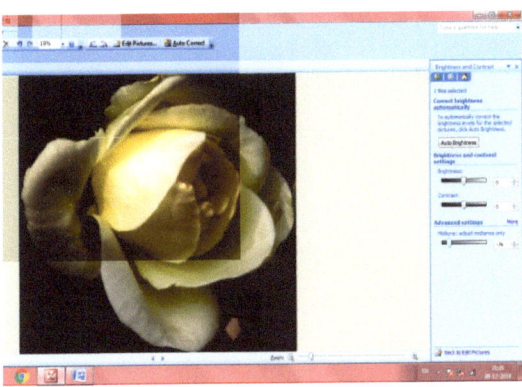

When the Mid tones are more, shades are almost washed away, as shown below.

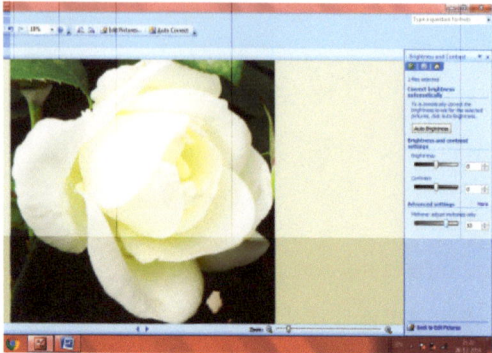

Close that window or click again the tab " edit photo". Then select color corrections. Here, by adjusting the three parameters called "amount", "hue" and " saturation" we can get different colored roses, starting with white rose.

That is illustrated in series of pictures below.

By combined adjustments, we can get green rose!

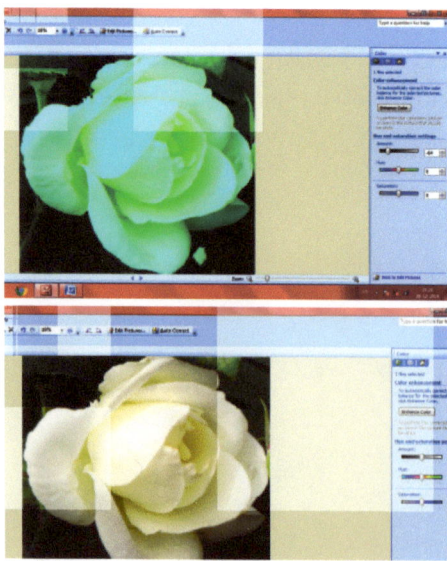

White rose above changed to pale red rose below.

Flower Photography

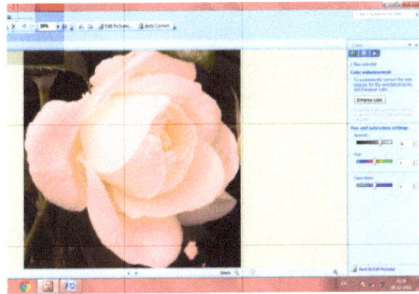

Next, saturation is made maximum, amount is less and hue is towards minimum results in yellow rose!

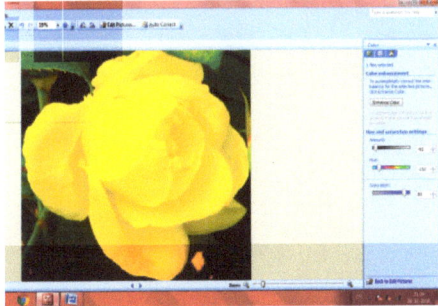

Editing in MS word!

Yes, we can do many corrections for picture in MS word itself.

Steps:

- Click to select the picture.
- Click "format"
- Then many options like " brightness", "contrast" and so on will be seen at the left hand top corner.
- Select the required thing and edit.

Jayaram as

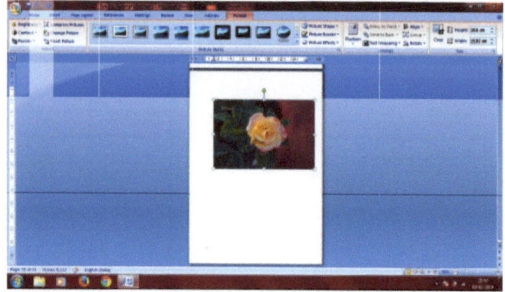

In the picture below, brightness is increased to 20%.

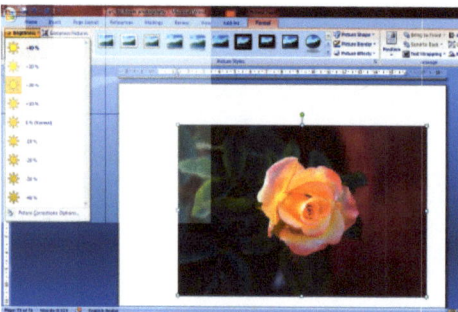

In the next picture, contrast is increased by 30%.

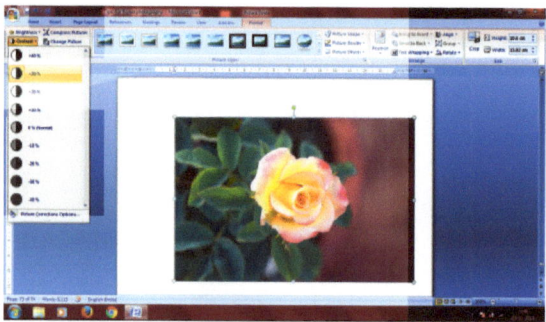

We can even crop or size the picture.

Editing in Picasa.

Steps:

- Select the picture and open it in Picasa.
- Select "edit in Picasa"
- Then the window will open with the

Flower Photography

selected photo and lots of parameters for editing.

- We can see on the right side all the information about the picture, including detailed settings of the camera.
- In the first menu, only brightness can be altered with cropping and a bit of color shades.

That is shown in the photo below.

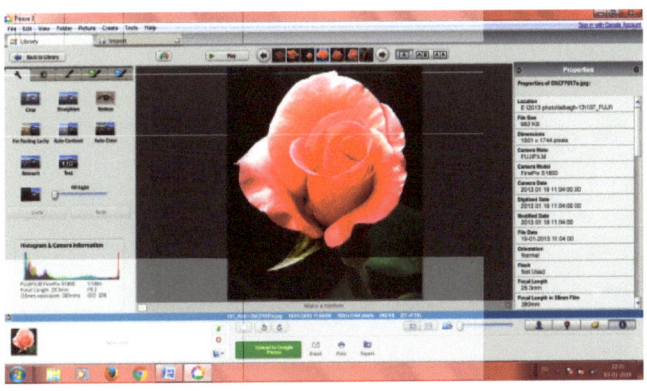

Next menu has many corrections on the left hand side of the screen.

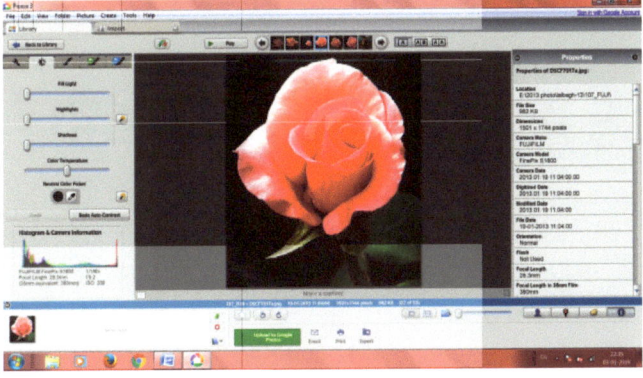

Compare the picture above and below. The back ground is made

55

dark, by operating " saturation".

Likewise, we can do many corrections.

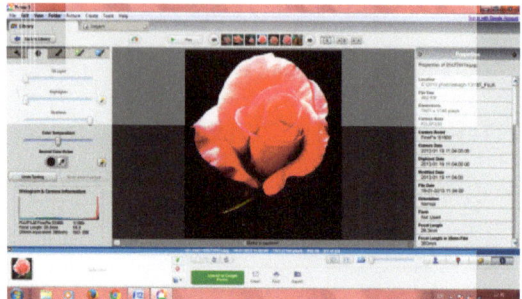

Next three menus will make different colors, effects like emboss, black and white, single color glow, invitation card like photo and so on. All these are shown in the following pictures.

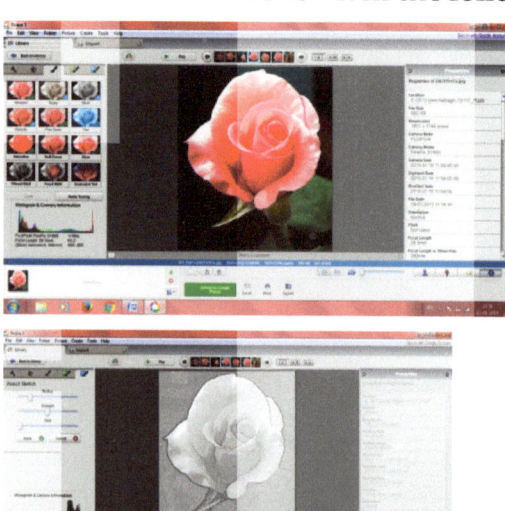

Flower Photography

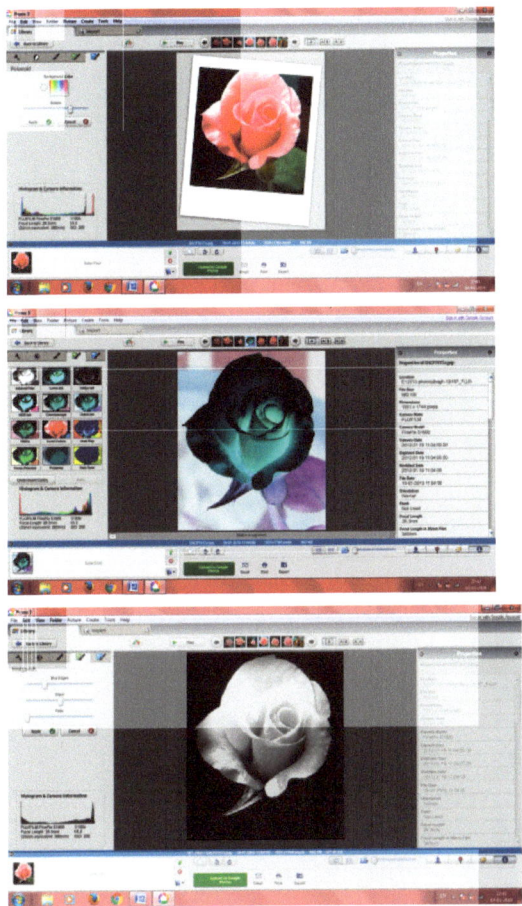

Editing with MS power point.

Steps:
- Open power point
- Start with blank option.
- Insert required picture
- Click "insert" and select" shapes"
- Insert arrow mark as shown and change

57

color, size and so on.

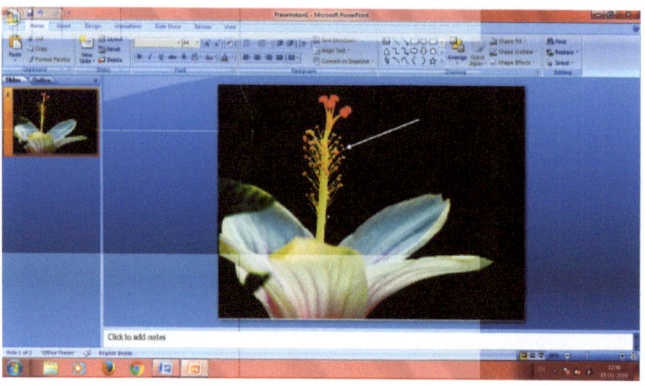

- Click " word art"
- Type the required text and adjust the size and font, color.
- Adjust the position of the text just at the end of the arrow tail.

The result is the picture shown below.

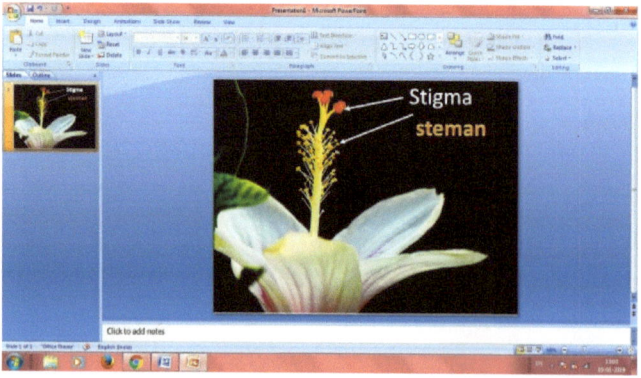

We can even place more than one picture side by side and save it as single jpeg picture.

Flower Photography

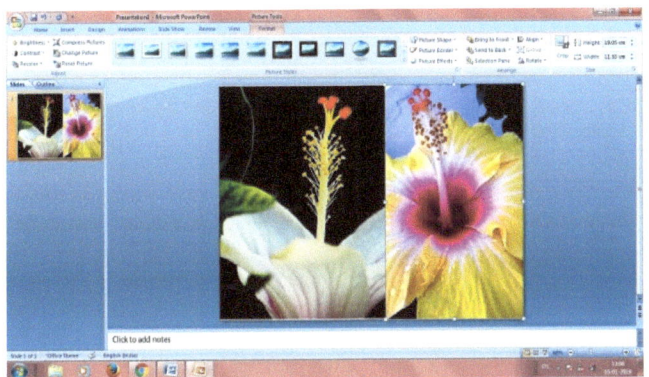

After selecting the picture, select "shapes". Then the picture will be enclosed in that shape! It is shown by picture inside the ellipse below.

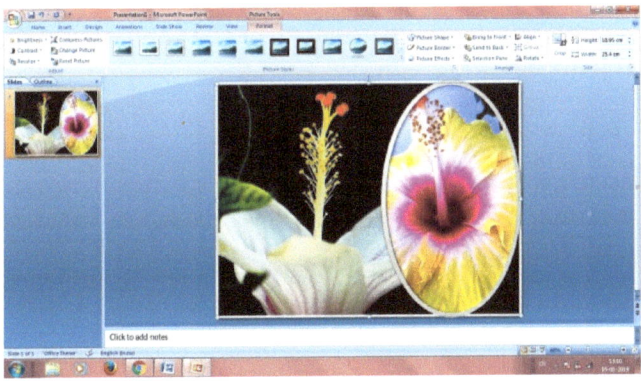

It can be even a 3d box, as shown below.

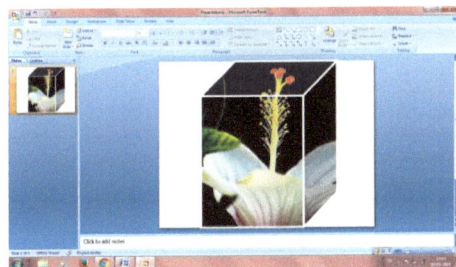

Arrow mark or a star as shown below.

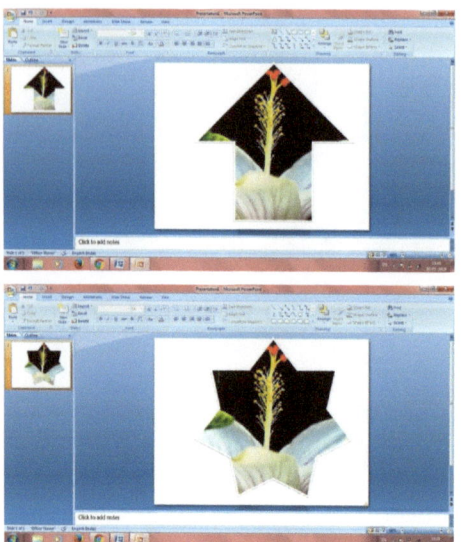

There is no limit for learning and there is no limit for art.

Best of luck.